SOCIAL MEDIA INFLUENCER

Learn Step-By-Step How to Build Your Personal Brand and Grow Your Business

BRYAN BREN

Thank you for downloading this book!

In order to thank you, **I would like to offer you a complementary download** about 5 social media marketing tips you should know before reading this book.

CLICK HERE TO GET IT AND STAY IN TOUCH

Table Of Contents

Introduction

In the world of today, social media influencers are increasingly becoming the most popular people in determining social, cultural, economic, and even political trends. However, growing an audience and becoming credible enough to exert some power through the Internet is an increasingly difficult thing to do. First off, the field is very crowded, with numerous influencers already commanding huge followings in most of the niche areas. When you start out, these influencers will also be better off than you in terms of social media followers as well as experience, which can make for a combination of factors that might scare you off.

Now, social media influencing is growing into a whole industry all by itself, meaning that influencers actually run businesses. Even though a lot of businesses use social media to reach their audiences and sell to them and institutions still communicate through social media to their followers, there is still lots of room for enterprising people to generate and sell their own authority in the socials. With a few thousand followers, you can operate your accounts as a medium for other businesses to advertise, making money much like television stations and other media.

However, you must realize that it is one thing to get a good following on Instagram, Twitter, or YouTube, but it is an entirely different matter to convert this following into cash. There really is no reason to become an influencer if you do not at least make some money off it. The dream, of course, is to make a good living through social media influencing. This is why this book is so important. You need to learn the dos and don'ts of the influencing world to make it in the highly competitive and fast-changing environment. I have divided the book into four parts, each one outlining the process of creating a living out of social media.

In the first part, you will learn all about branding. You must be careful of the kind of brand you make, because all industries are not equally lucrative. Some have greater opportunity for making money and others require a lot more work to succeed in. Knowing the right way to make a brand (and the right brand to create) will go a long way in determining the kind of social influence business you will succeed in creating.

The second thing that you must do is to build your audience. This is by far the most difficult and time-consuming part of the whole process. It will take months, possibly years of creating content and interacting with your followers before you get to the levels of followership that social media influencers require to make money. It is even more complicated because you have to keep an eye on your brand identity and another on the monetization that follows.

In most cases, you will start to make money from your accounts during the audience-building process. I mean, sites like YouTube pay content creators by number of views rather than subscribers, which is great. But to make some real money from social media influencing, you have to go further than the money that you get from adverts on your channels. You have to get into endorsement, affiliate marketing, merchandising, and other areas.

Every section is just as important as the rest, and if you mess up in one area, you will feel the repercussions across the board. So starting out it will be a tightrope walk figuring out what kind of brand you should create. After that, you must target a very specific audience to whom your brand will appeal and target them as followers. With a good enough following, you can then turn your attention to monetization, turning the views, likes, and comments you receive into Bitcoin and dollars to live off. And once you have reached this milestone, you must work just as carefully to maintain your brand and income streams.

Let me just take one moment to assure you that this book has been written based on information gathered from observation. I have analyzed the behaviors of some of the Internet's most influential celebrities, socialites, and influencers to create you the most genuine and effective process of getting into the influencing business. These strategies have been highlighted using real life and hypothetical scenarios to give you a better idea of how they would work.

You will not find the kind of content in this book anywhere else. The insights contained within these pages are fresh, they are brand new, and they work. If you read carefully about the lessons taught in the following four sections and execute them well, then I can assure you that you will succeed. Why? Because I have seen people use the exact same strategies and amass a huge following, improving their business' substantially in no time.

A few people have tried some of the strategies that I have outlined in the book. They have not caught on in the market, but they are bound to catch on in due time. Most are brand new tactics that I have come up with based on my own experiences with social media influencing.

Part 1: Create Your Brand

The brand is everything in the world of social media influencing. Without a good, stand-out brand, people will never be able to pick you out from the billions of other social media users. The journey to making money and running a successful online enterprise all starts with your brand. In this chapter, I will give you a few pointers about setting up a business in social media influencing.

Think of it as a Business

To command a good following and make good money, you must think about the whole process of becoming a social media influencer as a business. The product you sell is your clout and reach on various social networking sites. Other companies can sell their products, services, or information to the people you attract through your channels, making the followers both an audience and a commodity. Of course, you don't want to think of your followers as commodities, but an understanding of their role in your social media influencing business will go a long way.

The first thing you must do is define your brand as a social media influencer – this is your business. That short bio on every one of your accounts can be the difference between a user following and subscribing to your content and rotting in irrelevance. When you define your brand, you know what you stand for. Clarity goes a long way in empowering the hard work involved in the world of social media influencing.

Another thing you can do once you define what your social media accounts stand for is the followers and views milestones. This, in turn, informs the kind of content that you will create as well as the forms of outreach that you will use to attract followers. If you want to get numerous followers quickly, you will have to go for viral-worthy content. Even YouTube has milestone awards for it. The process of setting followers and views milestones for your accounts also calls for you to find out the kind of traction that accounts get as far as getting followers, views, and likes is concerned.

Because you will definitely have to promote your accounts and the content you create in the beginning, setting milestones is a budgetary concern as well. For example, with YouTube, a few thousand views for the first few videos you post is quite a tall order, unless it is viral content or you have a huge marketing budget and you promote it extensively. Otherwise, just using hashtags and optimizing your content to ongoing trends takes a lot more time.

Finally, thinking and operating your social media accounts as a business (or more like a business than a hobby) allows you to show up every day to do what you need to do. For most people, social media is something that you indulge in depending on your moods. However, anyone who knows anything about social networking knows that some times of the day are more lucrative in generating attention than others. So unless you can plan out your posting calendar, use scheduled posts, and be consistent in your activity, you will have difficulties generating any traction.

Stand Out

As I mentioned before, billions of people operate successful social media accounts. Hundreds of thousands aspire to be influencers, with a good number already commanding a respective following. You will have to go well out of your way to catch the attention of social media users. You have to make your brand pop and stand out. You have to be the unique one in an industry of copycats and rip-offs. Just think about it.

The best kind of an influencer is the one who can put him or herself in the shoes of his or her followers and fulfill their desires. In this case, the desire to access new content at all times, combined with the abhorrence of repetitive materials. So, think about the number of times that have you seen the same joke on two or more accounts online. In most cases, when something is trending (and sometimes when a picture, video, or meme is trending) you will see it in numerous accounts, unchanged, in the span of a few hours or days. When this happens, you will not even remember where you saw the video, meme, or picture the first time or the person who created it.

And if you are starting your influencer brand that you later hope to convert to a marketing outfit for other businesses and/or yourself to use to reach a specific market, standing out is absolutely essential. A user must be able to pick out your profile from the thousands of look-alikes. Your bio must cover their needs, and your content must fulfill their desires.

One strategy that I have seen working very well is that of actually standing for something. Instead of just being a needy social media user begging his or her followers to like or subscribe, give them a reason to do this. One effective tool to gain followers for YouTube content creators has always been that last part of every video. Everyone tries to find something creative to convince users to subscribe and "hit the notification button". Sure, sometimes the reminder is effective in reminding new users to do those things. But a lot of the times, the user will already have hit those buttons if they liked the content.

It is when you stand for something popular that you actually gain an advantage. It is when you, say, donate a dollar for every one hundred likes to some popular cause that people care about your channel. It is when your final message is simply a call to action on some issue that someone watching your video would be passionate about, do you actually get those likes, follows, and subscriptions. The heart and soul of your channel or account is what actually gets you those things.

Stand for Something

When you go even further along this path, you get into the popular issues of the day. You start talking about subjects that a big celebrity might see and actually endorse your brand by liking, following you, or even talking you up to his or her own followers. Imagine Beyonce giving you a shout-out because you are vocal about an issue about which she cares deeply. That would be huge! This is a very tentative strategy for generating a good following. You have to tread a very thin line between advocating for issues close to your heart, issues that people care about, and non-inflammatory content. With the last one, you might find yourself on the wrong side of a complaint to the networking site you are using to generate some traction for your brand.

In a less epic degree, you can stand for something even in the entertainment, fashion, and other less serious fields. The idea is to be the ultimate source of whatever content you provide your audience. For example, if you want to start an entertainment brand, you can be the source of a particular type of joke, like puns, imitation, sarcasm, etc. This is the first step in the journey to having a binge-worthy channel(s), something that we are going to talk about later on.

Make Sure You Choose Something You Love

The passion you have about a topic shows in everything that you do. The more passion with which you do something, the greater the impact it will generate. In the same manner, the more the impact of your content, the more money you will make off it. Therefore, it is essential to be involved in something at which you are very passionate. In social media influencing more than any other field, if you do what you love, you will never work a single day of your life. Even though you may set up your accounts in a business-like manner, you will be doing something you love and be paid for it.

So find those passions you have and put them to work in your social media accounts. PewDiePie is one of the most popular YouTube channels with over 100 million subscribers. Yet the kind of content you will find there is playful, even whimsical, ranging from games such as Minecraft, movie reviews, and anything else the vlogger cares about. The main thing that people are looking for on the Internet is a connection, and nothing resonates with people more than genuine passion. If you give your brand all your love and passion, people are bound to respond positively.

A lot of what you will be doing in your social media influencing career is inspiring others on a wide range of topics. For example, if your brand is all about exercise, you must be the most passionate person your followers know. You must be tireless, fanatical even, in everything that you do. When your followers look at your activity, they need to see the best possible version of themselves in you. Moreover, you simply cannot do that if you are just pretending to love what you do. Passion shows. And there is nothing worse than being seen to be faking it on social media. That is when the trolls come out in masses and make your life a living hell of negative comments and cruel jabs.

And passion inspires passion as well. If you are

dedicated to your craft, your viewers will pay back your dedication in kind. They will like, follow, and share. They will even talk you up to their friends. They will answer to every one of your calls to action. You will become their leader, shouting the war cry and leading them to battle on every promotion, every issue of importance, and every campaign. And if that is not real influence, then I do not know what is!

Insert Running Gags into Your Content

Anyone who has watched television understands the concept of running gags. They tie people together, creating a community that laughs about the same things, cares about the same things, and generally have a good time together. Well, you can apply the concept of running gags in social media as well. This is especially true for the video content that you create. These are inside jokes that make every one of your followers respond to your content. Even if you do not insert those jokes in every post, they will still bind your viewers into a community when you make them.

A running gag also makes your brand more relevant and recognizable. It is like your best friend or partner's personality quirks – they endear him or her to you. Running gags are an essential part of your brand because they create a distinctive identity for you. Your running gag can be a catchphrase, a facial reaction, a change in voice, etc. I have seen influencers who tell bad jokes and get very positive reactions, simply because their bad jokes are so bad. You just have to find that one thing, and a running gag is one of the best things that you can do.

Another reason why you should insert a running gag into your content is that running gags have more viral power. Even if it is just one of your posts with a running gag that goes viral, the people who decide to check out your account will decide to stay because they find more of the same. Then you can have your running gags become some sort of slow viral content produced regularly that keep your audience interested in you. Whatever the case, once an audience relates with your running gag and loves it, they will certainly become huge fans. This is the real capital for a social media influencer.

I have said it before and I will say it again; you have to think like a member of your audience to create truly successful content. Now, think like a follower and try to think about a time when you stumbled on an account and binged yourself into the night. What made you do that? Nine out of ten times, people binge because they have found so much of something they love that they simply cannot stop themselves. This is what a running gag does for you. Whatever running joke you decide to run with should be one that would make a person finding be captive to you for as long as it takes to finish everything you have created. If you exhaust one idea, move on to a related idea. It is not very hard to branch from one idea to another when you have been doing it for some time. You can then continue exciting your followers with quirky, standout jokes that keep them coming back for more.

Charisma

A charismatic influencer is an appealing influencer. Can you make someone change his or her mind because of something you did or said? Your brand will be more successful if you can figure out a way to do this. The best influencers have always been those who can figure out a way to make boring topics interesting enough that you take a moment to listen to them. In my analysis of the most outstanding social media influencers, I have noticed that it does not matter so much what you are saying to people as how you say it.

One of the most popular news-based YouTube channels is Last Week Tonight where host John Oliver talks about the most mundane issues in American life to his audience of over 7 million subscribers. Granted, he is a decorated professional comedian, but you have still got to respect the fact that he makes so many people care about topics like the Iran deal, elections in far-off countries, and the mundane aspects of the Internet. It is all about the charisma.

Audiences react more to lively, bubbly content than they do to subdued or sad tones. Your personal brand should be exquisite, even dreamy, to inspire people. This is the key ingredient in every celebrity brand out there. Charisma gives your brand a distinctive appeal, making it more personable and attractive. And like any other aspect of your brand, it is the content that will determine your level of charisma. The opening and closing remarks in every one of your posts are especially critical for this.

The graphics with which you set yourself apart; logos, headshot, color scheme, etc. also play a role in determining your brand's appeal. You will have to use a very different set of graphics to appeal to educated collegiate fans than you will need to appeal to teenagers. As long as you understand the demographic to which you are trying to appeal, you will be okay. It goes without saying, of course, that video content is very powerful as a tool for your brand's identity. Even if you just post a short Instagram video and pin it on top of your posts, people react better to motion graphics than they do to words or pictures.

The final reason why you should aim for a compelling brand is that the content you create will always have mass appeal. When you put yourself out there in every piece of content that you create for your fans, they will always reward you with massive shares and probably take your content viral. Aiming for a captivating brand forces you to go out of your way to please your fans. Now in real life, living to please others may be frowned upon. But when it comes to social media, the better you are at pleasing people, the more successful you will be. A carefully crafted personality rather than whimsical content strategy is the best bet you have of getting your brand to that position of having mass appeal. Unless part of your brand identity is whimsy, in which case you can keep posting on a wide range of topics and appeal to your fans in that way.

Split Personality Brands

When you read blog posts and other books about social influencers, you will find that they talk in large part about being authentic and real. "Bring out the real you," they say, without factoring in the fact that sometimes the "real you" is not very business-worthy. Let us be real. Not every one of us would appeal to the large number of people you need to start a social influencing business. I have also met many influencers who feel that the massive exposure their lives get from their social media accounts turns sour later on. Suddenly, you find that you don't want your satisfaction from something you did to be determined by the number of views and likes it got on social media. In fact, burnout from over-exposure is one of the leading causes of brand failure in the social media influencing industry.

Let us not forget the Internet trolls; those people whose sole purpose for existence seems to be to inflict the worst possible pain onto others. You can only take so many insults and abuse before you start to crack. When they are directed straight at the things you are most insecure about, then it gets even more serious. Nobody needs to be reminded about their worst flaws every day.

That is why the idea for split personality social media brands is so appealing. Here, you create some emotional distance between you and your brand. It becomes an extension of you, not the essence of you, which makes all the difference when you are dealing with trolls. Moreover, a split personality brand is easier to manage because it is just a part of you that you are sharing with the world. You can work on it to make it better over time, working tirelessly without burning out.

So to counter those who insist that you have to put all of you out there, let me just say that your brand does not have to have the same characteristics as you. Sometimes it makes more sense to create a completely new personality for your brand. It gives you greater creative freedom in generating content. Moreover, you can take it even further because your sole focus is on a very small part of you. For example, if, among other things, you love swimming, you can create a social media presence around the pains and joys of swimming. Between swimming wear, swimming lessons, swimming pool etiquette, and extreme swimming (oceans, waterfalls, height dives, etc.), you will have many areas to explore.

An added bonus to focusing on a single aspect of your life is that your fans will always be looking out for glimpses of your real life, creating a stronger brand. Later on, we will also look at the advantages of a specialized brand during monetization. I mean, think about it. In that example above, were you not already picturing the numerous brand endorsements that a brand like that could do? Would you have as clear a picture if that brand featured 20% swimming, 15% working out, 40% social life, and 25% school life? Of course not! But that swimming brand could easily be run by a student who parties and works out. You just have to figure out what areas of your life would have the greatest appeal and has stuff at which you would like to get better. There is nothing like likes, follows, and shares to get you working around the clock. If you can limit the areas of your life at which you are in a constant race to beat others (competing influencers), you will have found the perfect way to live your best life indeed.

Best Practices

I use Instagram in this section because it is the most influential of all social sites at the present. If you make it on Instagram, then you can make it anywhere. In fact, you can use these tips and tricks (with just the slightest of tweaks) on any other social networking site and they will work just as effectively.

Authenticity

People make a big deal out of being yourself in everything you post on social media, but that may not always be the case. If you are a social media entrepreneur using your social media accounts to exploit a business opportunity, being "the real you" may not always be very productive. What I would advise, however, is that you be authentic to the brand. If your brand is that of a person who posts about every area of your life, then you must be that person all the time.

It is all fine to open up your life to your followers and live it in the limelight – sharing everything all the time. But you can still be a social media influencer if that is not something you feel comfortable doing. Heck, you could go a long way as the premier source for cute animal videos, gaming tips, cool electronic gadgets, etc. Just be sure that you keep everything uniform and do not mix it up.

Themed Posts

There are people who are boring because they never do something worth getting excited about, then there are those who fail to impress because they are all over the place. Users relate best to content with a similar overarching theme. This further boosts your brand identity and allows your followers to relate with you on a deeper level.

Avoid Becoming a Spam Account

This is especially critical if you have developed an e-commerce website along with your social media accounts. It is okay to use your posts to send your followers to your e-commerce accounts, but you have to be very careful about this. Constantly bombarding your audience with promotions and offers often backfires, with followers becoming immune to your efforts and sometimes even unfollowing your account. The best way to sell is to have windows of commerce during which you open up your stores and focus on selling as much as possible.

For example, you can dedicate one week every month to selling and focus on generating hype for the sales week three weeks every month. By the time your items come out, your followers will be eager to go. Whatever efforts you put towards promoting sales week (including paid promotions and cross-promotions with other influencers) will be more effective in this window. Moreover, a shorter time selling the stuff that your audience craves allows you to capitalize on that sense of urgency to sell more.

Outstanding Content

I cannot insist on this issue strongly enough. Content is the most important weapon in the arsenal of a social media influencer. Content is king. Content is the subject. Content is everything. You must show fanatical dedication to generating the best possible content for all your social media accounts if you are to have a prayer of becoming the leading brand in your area of influence. As you think about and actually start your brand, keep in mind that of all the things you will have to do to build your brand, content creation will take the most time and have the greatest impact.

That is why it is always important to have a content

creation plan; a list of all the topics and sub-topics that you can explore in your field. As you do this, you will find new ideas to branch out of the main topics, sub-topics to expand to full topics, and sequels to the content to which your fans respond more favorably among others.

In the issue of content, one area at which most people mess up is the post-production editing. As a content creator, you will be trapped between two opposing and very powerful forces – the forces of authenticity that fans crave and those of glamour that they reward. If you veer too much in one direction, you will lose in the other end. You need both of these things to make it as a social media influencer. So, how do you find the perfect balance between glamour and authenticity without being boring or fake? Learn to use editing apps.

The use of filters, nay, the professional use of filters, is absolutely critical to the social media influencer. Take a course, if you must, but make sure that your filters game is flawless. You can open a practice account to learn the art of using filters before launching the real thing, or just ask your friends to judge your work. But, as much as possible, avoid posting photos and videos which are not 100% outstanding. The Internet is forever, after all, and you don't want those embarrassing photos cropping up just when you are about to sign a lucrative sponsorship deal.

Engage with Your Audience

The easiest way to do this is to just reply to comments. The more fruitful way is to give shoutouts to your most ardent followers. This makes them feel that they share in your success. You can also give your followers a task like sharing your content, with the best two or three getting a shoutout. This way, you give incentive to you most ardent fans to bring in more fans. You can go a long way with something like that.

Part 2: Build an Audience

For an influencer, the audience is both the client and the product. Businesses will pay you to sell to them, making them your clients/customers, but you must have them in large enough numbers for your services as an influencer to be sought out (the product). Obviously the more of them you have, the more profitable your career will be. The secret to building a profitable following on social is knowledge. You must have a proper understanding of what marketers need in a target market and the things that your audience might be interested in while searching for products and services on the Internet. In this section, we will look at all the things that you need to take care of to build your brand to the levels needed for monetization.

Target Mapping

In the preceding chapter, we touched on the idea of running your social media-influencing career like a business. Target mapping is one of the most no-nonsense strategies of building a network with the potential for conversion (into customers) later on. What you need to understand is that each of the major social networking sites (SNS) attracts a particular type of user. Even those people who are active on more than one SNS indulge different areas of their personality when they explore different social sites. For example, while YouTube is almost exclusively entertainment-centric, Twitter is the ultimate site for trending topics. Instagram, on the other hand, is a lifestyle SNS where everyone opens up their lives to the world.

The first aspect of target mapping, defining your ideal follower, lets you know what kind of people you should be targeting. For example, if you are starting a foodist brand, you must know the kind of person who would be interested in savoring different kinds of food as a hobby. You must create a complete profile to spell out the age bracket, median income, social background, etc. By the end, you must be able to see your ideal follower as clearly as if they already existed. Make use of the tools available for social media penetration mapping. A resource like Social Mapper allows you to figure out what sites appeal to your target market and, later on, helps you compare your social networks for depth of penetration and impact.

The second aspect of target mapping is figuring out on what social networks you might find that kind of person. It is not a very clear-cut distinction, but you must determine which SNS will be your primary media and the ones that will be auxiliary. The one with the largest number of people fitting your profile will be your primary, receiving the chief share of your attention, while the other(s), still important but obviously less impactful, bring up the rear. Determine the exact distribution of your target market across the different social networking sites and use this ratio to determine the distribution of your resources, both monetary and in terms of content creation.

Ideally, you should start out on two or three social sites. This way, you will be able to customize your content to all sites instead of just sharing links and appearing to spam your followers. More than this and you will not have the time to engage with all your audiences, less than that and you will be faced with the problem of having too small a target market. So, if your ideal follower uses Instagram, YouTube, LinkedIn, Snapchat, Twitter, Vine, Facebook and a few other minor social medias, target them on two or three of their most commonly used SNS. Preferably, one of these should be their primary social network.

And in keeping with the strategy of thinking ahead, a clearly defined market and presence on social sites makes it easier to work with your partners to create a marketing strategy. Businesses appreciate marketers who have a good grasp of the market dynamics. Since your role as a social media influencer will be that of marketer, mapping out a target market will just make you better at fulfilling your clients' needs. This can be a very lucrative edge over your competitors.

Another area where target mapping comes in handy is in setting your goals for the accumulation of followers and subscribers to your channels. Focus on the primary site for the ideal kind of follower but keep all other channels in mind. Determine the pace of influence gathered by other influencers targeting your ideal customer and adjust your own targets accordingly, making sure that you do not go too high or too low. It must be an attainable target, but one that forces you to go out of your way to achieve.

Site Integration

Every site has its strengths and weaknesses. To present your brand in the most comprehensive way possible, you must create a seamless transition from one to the other based on the needs of the audience. This seamless transition is made even more critical by the fact that every one of your sites presents you with a very good opportunity to increase traffic to its sister sites. You see, there are things that you can do on Instagram that you cannot do on Twitter, LinkedIn, or YouTube. Similarly, some things come out better on one site but are lackluster on other sites. Integrating is the only way for you to funnel users from one site to the rest of your network and ensure that you highlight the best of your brand.

So, how exactly do you integrate? After all, SNS companies are competitors who may not always allow for the integration of competing networks on their sites. For example, while Facebook and Instagram are sister sites with a complete suite of integration tools, Facebook competes with LinkedIn, YouTube, and Twitter.

One of the best strategies that you can employ to direct traffic from competing social sites with no integration tools is in the graphics. Every SNS has a large billboard in the form of a header. This is what people see as soon as they click on your profile. A uniform header across all your sites makes your accounts very similar and easily identifiable. You must also try to make sure that the same username goes on all sites. This takes care of the searches that someone might do on a new site when they are looking for you on other platforms. Therefore, if a person searches for you on Instagram with the name you have used on your Twitter handle, they should have no trouble finding you.

Finally, as much as you should customize content across the different sites, make sure that you update all new information in each. This is especially important for the feeder platforms. If you are offering a giveaway on Instagram, both your Facebook and Twitter audience should know about it. As long as you do not make the mistake of posting links to one site from another site (giving the impression of being a spam account), your promotions across the different platforms should work very well.

Experiment with Content

The overarching theme in content creation is curiosity. The level of popularity that your content will generate will depend entirely on the amount of curiosity that the things you post generate in the target audience. The same trick has been used by movie trailers to build interest in movies and generate billions of dollars for single movies in some instances. But like the movie industry, it is not enough to make people curious. You must reward this curiosity with great content that will make the audience show interest in what you have to say and keep them coming back for more.

But you do not have to stick with one medium of communication to arouse (or hold) the interest of your followers. There are different types of content that you can use to communicate with your followers. The choice of what you use should depend on which one works best for the kind of information you are trying to send and the audience you intend to reach. In this section, we will evaluate the different types of content that can be used in any one of the mainstream platforms like Instagram, Facebook, LinkedIn, and Twitter. They include videos, pictures, infographics, and text. You must choose carefully depending on the kind of users that you want to attract.

Videos

Video content is one of the most efficient mediums for passing on marketing information. It has been proven that video content generates a lot more interest than any other medium. But there is a catch – your videos must be interesting enough to capture and keep the attention of whoever is watching them for the duration. Short videos of below two minutes in length have been found to have the greatest impact, mostly because of the massive competition that exists for the attention of Internet users. More than 700,000 hours of content is posted on the Internet every day, with brands competing with entertainers, musicians, homemade videos against professional, and everything in between.

The main draw of video content (for the creator) is the sheer volume of information that you can pack into one video. You can use a voice over, actions, and conversations to set the scene, give information, and communicate very efficiently with your audience.

Another thing to love about video content is that it is easier for the users to consume. People love watching stuff a lot more than they love reading. A video will attract a lot more attention simply because all a person needs to do is click on it and nod, laugh, or think along with whatever information you are broadcasting.

Keep in mind that with video content, you only have the first fifteen seconds or so to make your impression. People usually watch for long enough to decide that a video is interesting. If they decide that it is not, they will move on to the next one. So be careful what you do with your first fifteen seconds because they will determine how many people watch the whole thing. However good your salutation or opening sequence might be, new viewers will bolt if they think you are wasting their time. Because here is an interesting fact; people use social media to get entertained even when they should not (basically to waste time) but they don't want to have someone waste their time with useless information.

Of course, there are a few challenges to video content. For one, it requires some specialized skills to create. If you don't know how to operate a video camera and edit video footage, you will probably have to pay someone to do these things for you. Otherwise, you will end up posting subpar content that does nothing for your brand.

Text

Text is kind of an old school way of communicating. The written word is quite a powerful tool for communication. Text only posts, however, may not be very effective in the highly competitive world of social media. When you are competing with cat videos and flawlessly filtered Instagram posts, you find that text may not be the most effective tool in the current times. Unless you are on Twitter, it is always better to spruce up your videos with some graphics.

Pictures

A single picture tells the story of a thousand words – so the saying goes. Pictures are the building blocks of Instagram, an important aspect of Facebook, and necessary to give Twitter posts an extra boost. Moreover, pictures make for a more interesting process of telling a story. In news, headline pictures generate interest and traffic. For personal accounts, the pictures you post will determine the kinds of followers that you attract.

Infographics

Infographics are an interesting way of presenting very serious information by putting it into picture form. Information presented through infographics is usually very serious, hard to derive from written text, but of critical importance. For example, if you are attending an event and need to advertise to your fans, or you are holding a sale and need to communicate the same, infographics come in handy.

Matching Content to Platform

You must match each type of content to the social media platform for which it is best suited. Other than YouTube that uses video exclusively and Pinterest that is an exclusively pictorial platform, the rest allow for the combination of various mediums of communication. It is advisable that you stick with the visual mediums like videos and photos, as these attract and retain the viewers' attention best.

However, because of the great impact that videos generate, you may want to lean on your video content a lot more than the other mediums. Learn video-making skills if you must, but be sure to have videos as part of your social media presence. Preferably, make videos your main tool for the creation and propagation of social media content. You will find that along with generating more traffic, it gives you a lot more freedom to express your brand personality.

Convert Fans into Super Fans

While you work to generate content for your different social media platforms, ensure that you focus on appealing to the emotions of your audience. Give them the kind of impactful content that converts them into your brand ambassadors, sharing and bringing other followers to your accounts. Forget viral content and focus on building a following. It is a lot more lucrative to have a total of ten million YouTube views of a hundred videos than it is to get one video that goes viral and generates ten million views while your other videos have a lot less viewers. You can build on the former and attract sponsors, but with the one-hit wonder situation, the success of your one video will overshadow your own efforts. Influencers who have gone the furthest have always been those who succeeded in getting their followers to recommend their brand to a few close friends who then become fans.

Focus on creating a community instead of an audience. Not only does this make you a lot more committed to the job, it gives you a huge head start in beating your competition. So how exactly can you do this?

First off, you must appeal to the fantasies of your followers. What makes them tick? What do they all care about? This, of course, is something you already figured out while creating your personal brand. When it comes to making super fans out of your fans, you must be the most idealized version of what they are looking for. If someone is interested in working out, they should use you as an example of a great trainer, dedicated weight lifter, or yogi. If someone loves swimming, make sure that they give you as an example when telling their friends about the best swimmers they know. You do not have to have won a medal or even participated in any major sports (this might actually disqualify you) to become the idealized version of your niche market.

All you need to do is appeal to fantasies.

Secondly, you must be careful how you communicate. Anything you put out onto your social media platforms must build to your idealized image. Vet every little piece of information about you that your followers see, including what your fellow influencers are saying about you. If it ever comes to it, ensure that you also scrutinize what the mainstream media says about you. Having a strong base is all about limiting access to you, which in social media is all about the pictures, videos, and texts that are written about you.

The third thing that you must do is create a level of mystique around your brand. This means using teasers and cliffhangers to drum up interest in your personal life, then ensuring that you remain mum about it. This works best for those influencers who have only shared a small part of their lives with their fans. In that one area, everything may be out there and people may be able to find any information about you that they need. But about all other aspects of your life, keep a tight lid on it. This includes dating life, religious and political views, personal lifestyle, etc. As long as you impress and generate a massive enough following with your main thing, you will generate a lot of buzz any time a small detail of your life behind the curtain comes to light.

The fourth thing to keep in mind is that you should not try to appeal to everyone. You can only impress so many people even with targeted content in a very small niche of your demographic. Therefore, whatever your brand identity is, pursue that to the best of your ability and attract the people who are actually impressed by that kind of thing. You must be authentic to your brand identity and it should inform everything you do. The people who follow you because they identify will stick with you because you represent a part of themselves that no one does. Creating a super fan is all about giving your brand the authority that allows you to make recommendations for other businesses later on and actually have people buy.

Create Content that People Would Miss

The best way to build your audience is to appeal to them using quality content on all of your social media platforms. The idea is that a user would like your content so much that they look past all other distractions on the Internet and visit your profile repeatedly. This calls for you to set yourself apart from the rest of your niche with fun and impactful videos and pictures. Your focus should be on attracting lifetime followers, with milestones starting from one thousand to the ultimate aim of hundreds of thousands and millions – the figures attained only by the most serious influencers. To do this, you must:

Come up with a posting calendar and checklist. In establishing a serious social media influence brand, there is no use in posting ten times in one day and then going for a week without posting anything. It is much more profitable to have a fixed content distribution strategy. For example, you can design a content strategy in which you post one or two photos (or videos) every day, preferably at around the same time so that your followers can find them more easily. A content checklist will allow you to tick off the qualities you hope to achieve with each post. For example, if you're interested in directing attention towards e-commerce platforms (yours or those that you are being paid to promote), you should post at around the peak shopping hours. That way, if you come up with recommendations that benefit a person, he or she can come back whenever they want to get a similar experience.

In creating content, you must keep in mind the other influencers targeting the same market as you. These people will be looking to take your followers' attention and loyalty away from you. This is why you must be the first person to fulfill your follower's needs. If someone visits your platform looking for the motivation they need to hit the gym, or lessons for swimming, or just a dose of entertainment, they should find it. Your content must fulfill the needs of your fans. This, of course, goes back to the whole idea about understanding the market and creating a great brand, but you must keep people coming back for more.

Social media is all about never-ending consumption of content, so you should never sleep on the job. You must always remain relevant to your fans insofar as content consumption is concerned. That is to say that when new trends hit the market, you must adopt and be the one to introduce your followers to them. You should make sure that your followers can trust you to not just provide them with current information, but also update them with new trends. You must indulge people's interests to make them engrossed in your brand enough to follow your activity on all your channels. Stay ahead of the curve when it comes to trends in your field. When you have enough authority, go ahead and set the trends yourself. The earlier you start to exercise your strength as a social media influencer, the stronger you will become overall as a brand.

To ensure that you maintain the overarching theme of your brand, you must ensure that, especially when creating video content, you adhere to a well-crafted script. A script gives you much greater creative control of your content because you decide what to insert rather than just going with the flow, because sometimes what you want to say is not in line with your brand. More than that, a script allows you to sound exactly how your brand should sound, allowing you to maintain uniformity not just across the platforms, but between different posts as well. If you create a good enough script, it will allow you to grow your brand on your own terms, determining the direction of every aspect of your brand personality. This level of creative control is what keeps your followers glued to your platforms.

Finally, missable content combines the brand qualities of charisma and running gags. These are the exact things that followers look for when they come back to watch your old videos again, look at your old pictures, and laugh at those old jokes. But let me introduce a new concept in the creation of exceptional content: the signature. This can be a catchphrase, a sign, a sound, even a dance move, that is unique to you. It must be something that you have perfected, and you must give it that zing that makes people admire, even imitate you. The moment of magic is usually a split second, and running gags, signature, and charisma are the safest bets in achieving that. People might even consume your content just to hear you close with a signature they love watching you do. I know I have a couple of channels that I watch for the creator's charisma and signature move; in my case, running karate chops executed perfectly at the start and end of every video. As I said, the magic is all in the small things.

Influence the Influencers

Of all the followers that you will attract to your platforms, none will be quite as lucrative as another influencer. It is true that your social media profile will gain as much prominence as its biggest followers. Social media companies all have that tendency of telling the world who your most popular follower is. What many people don't appreciate is the level of influence that that small aspect of your account has. A lot of the time, people make the decision whether to follow you based on the people in their networks who follow you. If you get followed by a person with a large following, your profile will appear on the recommended follows list of more people. This gives you a great opportunity to reach and appeal to a bigger group of people than you would if your account did not get a big follower early on.

In this chapter, we will look at all the reasons why you must enlist the services of a social media influencer to build your own audience and become an influencer in your own light. It is a somewhat cyclical relationship, but I have seen it work in very many cases. An account will be having trouble penetrating the anonymity of newness, struggling with new followers, when a big name follows and sends it rocketing to the top of the charts. So, what can you do?

Well, I say do whatever it takes to get a big follower early on, including paying an influencer to follow you. There is no shortage of influencers to provide you with this exact kind of service. For a few hundred bucks, you can earn your platform(s) thousands of new followers and massive exposure. Just make sure to get an influencer with the same kind of target market as your brand, because a mismatch will bring you lackluster results. This is called a quid pro quo following, and you will probably find yourself doing the same thing later on in your influencing career. Let me issue a word of caution on this strategy though; beware of bots. These are computer-generated accounts that are automated to follow an account or drum up interest in a topic. Even though they are quite effective in improving the number of followers you account seems to have and the likes your posts get, they do not amount to genuine influence. Avoid the temptation to swell up your following with them at all costs.

Take advantage of follow trains to get in touch with

the more active spheres of social media. As you gain some prominence, start your own follow trains and promote these as a way to gain followers. A hashtag with your name on it that is used by thousands of people to gain more followers will set you up as an influencer a lot faster than settling on attracting one new follower at a time. With this, you will attract the attention of other influencers and increase your chances of being followed by someone of real import.

Another way to influence the influencers to build your audience is by creating targeted content. You can find the interests of the most popular people on social media quite easily. So easily in fact that you can customize your content to appeal to them. When you do this, you will increase your chances of attracting them to your platforms as a part of your following. This is how a lot of super fans for some of the world's biggest social media influencers have attracted the attention of their idols and gained massive traction in their own brands. It is a form of brand endorsement, except that in this case the purpose is solely to build an audience, not to sell merchandise or convince people to get some service.

Boost Your Reach

Many social media influencers shy away from promoting their content, partly because they feel that doing so will reduce their authenticity. A lot of people advocate for the natural growth style of building an audience in which you refrain from using money to promote your brand. But I insist that boosting your posts goes a lot further in taking you to the right place than a lot of these "organic" strategies. I do not mean to say that it is necessary for you to promote, but it might be the easier of all available tools. But even if you choose to refrain from paid adverts for your posts, there are a few things that you can do to give your content a little more life. In this section, we will look at some of these ways.

Paid Ads

There is no questioning the effectiveness of paid ads in generating traffic for your content and increasing the outreach of your brand. Social networks use some of the most sophisticated algorithms to take your content to the very people you need to view it, charging you for every engagement generated for your video, photo, or text post. With paid ads, you are assured of a fixed number of engagements. You also have greater control over who sees your brand.

If you are running your social influencing career like a business, paying to promote your content is just something you must do. In fact, it would not be out of the ordinary for you to have a budget and create a spending plan.

Using paid ads, you can either promote your overall brand to increase its overall reach or promote your content. Both of these strategies have their strengths and weaknesses, but the scales tip more towards the ideal of brand promotion. When you do this, you will generate interest for your whole business rather than a small aspect of it. Promoting just one post creates a situation in which you might have a single post with massive impact followed by lackluster posts afterwards. With promoted content, the competition is much greater, and because people are probably just skimming through, the risk of being passed over increases substantially.

Time Your Posts

Another great way to boost your reach is to time your posts. There are certain times when traffic to social networks is greater. These are the best times to post. You can use site aggregation services like Hootsuite and Google Analytics to find out the best times to post content online based on each social network's peak times. Once you have figured it out, create a posting timetable with reminders to create content and post it at the right moments. This will improve your predictability as a social media professional as well as the reach that your posts generate.

Best Practices

In this section, we will look at some of the best practices in the building of an audience of a social media brand. We will touch on imaging, retargeting, ways to boost inter-channel followers, super fans as brand ambassadors, the use of money for advertising, using social groups to expand your reach, and ways through which you can introduce the personal touch for greater impact.

Create a Consistent Visual Image

Image is key and you cannot survive as a social media influencer without it. It is absolutely essential for the well-being of your brand that you be consistent across different social media platforms. And when it comes to building an audience, this particular aspect of your brand becomes even more crucial. People will relate more with a very well designed visual image and attribute more credibility to it than a social media presence that is a lot more scattered. So, make sure that your headers on Facebook, Twitter, Instagram,

YouTube, LinkedIn, and any other social media account are the same. A video header is best for a consistent visual image. The photos that you will use on those headers can easily be snapshots of the video.

Retarget Your Audience on Different Social Media Accounts

There is a new trend in social media influencing where people try to create domains of influence in every social media platform. This is done as an alternative to combining all your followers into one giant pot and integrating. While it requires a lot more work to keep tabs on every one of your channels, the benefits you reap in terms of influence and audience numbers can be quite huge. However, when you decide to retarget your audience, then you must be sure to take one social media platform at a time. Trying to gain massive prominence on more than one social media platform is inadvisable because it might deny you the very opportunity you need to make an impression.

Reward Your Super Followers

As you grow your influence and increase the number of people who follow you, you will start to have a greater understanding of the people who make you successful. These include those who follow you in every one of your channels, people who always react positively to your calls for action, and those who engage with you and others. The best people to reward would be those who share your content with others. A simple shout-out is enough to excite a super follower and increase the chances of him or her becoming a loyal follower for life. In simple terms, rewards make your audience feel like they are a part of your team, which, in most cases, is all it takes.

Have Some Brand Ambassadors of Your Own

Brand ambassadors are the ultimate super followers. They engage with you on everything, share all your content widely, and bring in new people to follow you. And the best thing about all this is that you do not have to pay them to do all this! You can issue a call to action through your content for your existing followers to bring in more people. When enough of your followers respond positively, they can have a real impact on the number of followers your accounts garner.

Use Money to Reach Your Audience Where You Might Find It

Social media providers are more capable of reaching your target audience than you will ever be, so making them work for you to find your audience is an opportunity that you should take. The only way to do this (other than the free suite of tools that everyone else uses and thus grants you little advantage) is to pay to have your account showcased in prime places on the platform. For example, you can pay to bump up your account on the suggested follows list. This increases the number of new followers who see your name and boots your chances of getting new followers.

Use Already Existing Groups

This is one of the most effective but often overlooked strategies. You see, people join groups because they genuinely care about something. So if you are opening a fitness brand, hunt for new followers in those public groups. The same goes for sports accounts, entertainment, politics, or even news. It is not really poaching because these groups are free for all – I like to think about it as more of shooting fish in a barrel.

Exploit Personable Platforms

Most social media influencers are afraid to get too personal with their followers. They maintain a professional distance and avoid any personal touch. This may be easy, but it sure is not a very clever strategy. People respond to personal touch more than they do to empty words and content created for tens or hundreds of thousands of followers. WhatsApp is one of the best platforms for interacting with your followers on a more personable level – use it! WhatsApp groups are so much more effective for influencers because they make it easier for you to communicate with your audience right in their personal spaces.

Part 3: Monetize the Brand

After building the best brand and accumulating a big enough audience, you now get to the part where you start making money off your labors. It takes some time before you can start making money, anything from a few months to a year, which gives you the chance to accumulate some influence. In fact, trying to make money off your followers too quick has been found to be one thing that really slows down the careers of social media influencers. When you start selling or monetizing your social media accounts in any way too soon, followers get the impression that they are only as valuable to you insofar as they make you money. This is not something you want to have your fans feeling. You want to make them feel valued, interconnected, and appreciated. The first few months of your career should be all about making some connections, having fun, or pursuing whatever common interests your brand represents.

The most successful monetization efforts are those that seem to come naturally. For example, people have been asking you the secret to your great video or picture quality and you disclose that you use a particular phone type or some specific software for editing; whatever endorsement you can put together. To make the transition to monetization even more swift, you got this great deal whereby your followers can get, say, 5% off if they use a coupon that you are giving out. And right there, you gain the first advantage that makes social media influencers such successful marketers: you give your audience a better deal. Because of this, they not only trust you more, but you become the person who saved them some money. You cement their trust in you and at the same time, you make some money!

But it is not that simple. Oh, no. Monetizing a social media account(s) can be one of the most unpredictable things ever. In this chapter, we will talk about the process of monetization in detail. We will look at some of the things that you can do before you start monetizing, the actual process of monetization, and the various ways that you can make money off your followers.

Things to Note

There are a few things that you can do to make sure that your social media influencing career is as successful as it possibly can be. Let us say that you start the process of monetization after you hit ten thousand followers – the lowest number at which your followers allow you to actually have an impact. What are some of the rules that you must observe then?

The 70/20/10 rule

Well, first, you must balance between the different types of content that social media influencers post on their platforms. First, you have the original content you create specifically for your platforms. This includes videos, pictures, infographics, and text posts we discussed in the previous chapter. It should adhere to your brand identity, including the running gags and charisma that keeps your fans and followers coming back for more. Then you have the content that you share from other social media users (including your followers). These should be general interest pieces that will bring you more traffic or simply posts that you endorse. Even before you start monetizing, endorsing posts on social media by sharing on your platforms (and the massive activity that it generates for the original creator) is how you flex your influencing muscles. Finally, we have the content that you will only start introducing to your fans when you have determined that there are enough of them to monetize. This is called sales content and it includes material that is meant to convince your followers to make some purchase decision that benefits you. We will discuss the range of channels through which this may be achieved.

So, how do you determine the amount of content that should go into all these groups? Well, that could be very easy if you used the 70/20/10 rule. This means that 70% of what you post should be original content in line with your social media brand, 20% should be reposted content from other social media users, and 10% should be material meant to convince people to buy from you. Ten percent is all it takes. If you need to go past that to generate sales, then your brand is not ready to be monetized. Incidentally, it probably will not work anyway. Anything above 10% of marketing content makes your brand feel like a spam account, brings down the levels of engagement, and reduces your level of influence considerably.

And because I have already talked about original content, let me touch on the importance of the 20% part of that equation. This should strictly be affiliated brands and influencer content that you think would influence your followers. In fact, let me just spell it out. There is only one rule to social media influencing. That rule is: everything you do, you do it for your followers. They are the most important part of your brand. I know that there is a temptation to think that you would just make new followers if they left, so they are not all that important, but the truth is that they actually own you. You owe everything to your fans. And when you start trying to make money off them, this truth will become even more clear to you.

So use that 20% to appreciate your followers. Give shout outs, recognize them by reposting their stuff, and meet with them if you can. Anything you can do to make them feel special, do it. Because ultimately, the success of that 10% of marketing content that you post will be determined as much by the original 70% of original content as by the 20% of affiliated content that appears on your platforms.

Chatbots

If it were possible, any social influencer of merit would respond to every comment they received from their fans. But when you start posting frequently and the number of comments increase, it becomes harder and harder to reply to each comment. After all, you do have things to do, like creating more content and living your life. But private messages are a whole other thing. You miss out on a lot when you neglect your inbox, and not just from admiring fans expressing romantic interest or trolls just out to make your day terrible (thank God for those missed troll messages, right?). I am talking about the serious fans who will often flock your inbox to gush over their love for you. The level of attention you show them is often the make-or-break between lifetime super fans and a former fan who thinks you are too haughty for your own good. But then again, you might be getting too many messages to give each one of them your individual attention.

And that is where chatbots come in. Generally, people find it less demeaning to receive a generic, template message promising a later response than silence. The good thing about chatbots is that you can customize what they say to different messages based on the keywords used and the level of prominence of the person who texted. By using highly advanced artificial intelligence, a chatbot could even send messages better than you would.

Now let us talk about the situation when you start monetizing your social media accounts. Whatever channel you settle on, you will have to deal with followers asking you a range of questions as a part of their making a decision to engage. During monetization, every private message to which you fail to respond is a potential sale lost, a potential referral from which you would have made money that you did not complete, or a genuine customer concern that turns a potential repeat buyer away.

I cannot insist this enough, but you must respond to every private message your followers send you. It is critical to the monetization process. People are becoming increasingly shy of making public comments, especially about private matters, yet they still need to communicate and make their needs known. You must do everything you can to provide a safe environment for your followers to make their comments known to you. And one key ingredient in this process is the use of chatbots to reply to messages. This allows you to reap the benefits of being a keen listener (the loyalty and the dollars of your fans) without necessarily spending the whole day replying to messages.

The good thing about bots is that you can send batch responses to similar questions and the bot will tweak them to make them even more personable. With a chatbot, your response rate could be 100% of 50% of the effort needed to reach those levels. Considering that private messaging plays such a critical role to money making among social media influencers, you would be very remiss to let such a great opportunity pass you by.

Monetization Channels for Social Media Influencers

Now that we have laid the groundwork for the monetization process of your social media accounts, let us look at the exact ways that you can make money from those followers you worked so hard to attract.

Influencer Marketing

Influencer marketing is the most obvious way of monetizing your social media following. In this case, you simply give businesses access to your network for them to send marketing information and make buyers of them. This works much like television stations, except that the business will usually do their due diligence to determine the kind of following that you have. For the business, the advantage of social media influencer marketing is that it gives them the chance to reach out directly to their most probable buyers. Unlike television that reaches people in the target group and a lot of those who are not, social media brings together people of similar interests. For example, Sony Games will make a lot more headway marketing to gaming fans on similarly affiliated channels. Moreover, the capital investment needed for social media advertising is much less compared to running TV ads.

Understanding your position in the order of things

will make you a better influencer. But how exactly do you do this?

Work Behind the Scenes

The process of finding businesses and products to endorse on your channels is usually like the duck whose feet work furiously under the water while swimming but appears to be doing nothing of the sort above the water. You must start working on attracting businesses in need of influencers even before you get into it. You must establish a connection, a talking relationship, even offering free publicity earlier on as you build up your audience. For example, if you are running a gaming brand, make sure that you are in touch with the makers and/or marketers if the games you play as you create content for your growing fan base. Ask for technical clarification, manufacturer secrets, and design comparisons with competitors – anything to help you establish a working relationship.

The businesses will probably reach out to you to

suggest that you start marketing their products. After all, businesses today understand the impact of social media influencers. They know that if they do not offer you a deal, a competitor will move in and sweep you up. This is why social media influencing is a full-time job. When you are not busy creating content, you are engaging with your fans. When you are not doing either of these things, you are taking care of the business side of your career.

Like I said before, the people who succeed in creating profitable social media influencing ventures are those who do it like a business, putting in the commitment and dedication that an entrepreneur puts in a business to everything that they do. Even with a very specialized niche market, you cannot wait for the marketers to come to you. There will always be other influencers, maybe some who have more influence than you do, and it is your job to convince the marketers that their interests would be better served with you than with anyone else.

Your business becomes a full-blown business just like that, complete with a front-end operation of taking content to your customers and the back-end that entails the soliciting of service seekers. If you are not capable of taking care of both areas of your operation at the same time, you can even get a person who is better qualified to do these things for you. This leaves you with all the time you need for the generation of content and solicitation of followers.

Converting Your Followers' Trust into Purchase Decisions

Whether you have been entertaining them for a few months now or you have been giving them beauty tips, you have to ease into the monetization aspect of the brand. However loyal your followers are, they will still need to be convinced to go in the direction you will be pointing them to. It is not enough to recommend a certain product. You must give reasons why purchasing it is the best decision for your audience. Here, you have to show the strengths of your recommended product, comparing it with others and selling it on its advantages.

As much as social media marketing gives businesses a channel to make direct sales and a host of product ambassadors at a low price, it has also evolved to become the competition of the superior. You see, people are more liberal in their views and with a simple product review, any weaknesses in a product will be broadcast to the whole wide world. Whatever your level of influence, you should never try to convince a person to buy a product of poor quality.

The outcome can only be either one of two things: your follower practices their right of choice and decides to go with a different product. The business for which you are advertising ends up advertising for their competitors. Your reputation as an influencer suffers irreparably and your social influencing career ends even before it starts. Alternatively, a follower takes your word for it and buys a poor quality product. They lose confidence in you and never follow your advice on anything else. This makes you an ineffective influencer with no real power.

The best form of influencer marketing is the type that entails discovering little-known brands of high value and taking them to the world. This is doubly beneficial in that your fans (and the rest of the Internet) will recognize your expertise as an influencer and as the ultimate authority on the best products in your niche. Every good review for the product will become a great review for your brand. On the other hand, businesses will recognize your power to influence buyers and drive sales. You can then sell your services at a premium to the highest bidder. This is exactly what a social media influencer's life should be like.

You must be willing to go the extra mile and do the extra work that will allow you to uncover the hidden gems of the Internet. Vet the products you market extensively and critically, recommending only those that meet the highest standards of quality to your followers. This is the assured strategy to make it in influencer marketing as a beginner. You start with the unknown brands, gain your reputation, and make your way over to the big leagues making deals with multinational brands. And as you build your profile and advance up the ladder, the amount of money your social accounts generate for you will rise right up alongside you.

Marketing Through Lifestyle
The influencer's lifestyle is one of the most lucrative avenues for money making. You see, as an influencer, you will be acting as a role model to other social media users on specific issues. Therefore, if you recommend something that you are already using, people will respond more favorably. That is how influencer marketing works in a nutshell.

A rising trend on lifestyle endorsement is informing your audience where you got the material you use to create content. Just by mentioning a business or a brand, you generate massive interest among your followers. To market through your lifestyle, be prepared to open up your whole life to your followers. Everything you wear, every place you visit, every product you use will all be scrutinized.

But nonetheless, lifestyle marketing is one of the most lucrative strategies of making money as an influencer, especially for those who have massive followings and clout. Sadly, this is almost always not the case for you when you have been working to build your social media influencing business from scratch. This moneymaking avenue will open up to you much later.

Generate Leads for Other Websites

You can also use your influence to generate traffic for other websites through your platforms. On some channels like Facebook, you can even insert website links on the images that you post. Anyone viewing the content you post can then be redirected to the host website. Lead generation may be used along with other strategies to generate revenue for your business. In most cases, lead generation is packaged as part of a sponsorship deal with a particular brand.

Sponsorships

Sponsorship deals are some of the most lucrative sources of money for celebrities, even outside of the social media influencer circles. From sportspeople to singers, actors, and socialites, getting paid to have your brand associated with a particular product has always generated the more influential members of the society a ton of money. This is old news, of course, and you probably have a long way to go before you are popular enough to be the brand ambassador for a huge company like Nike or Coca Cola. Smaller brands that you are better suited for rarely ever engage the services of brand ambassadors. Nevertheless, you can still make a lot of money through sponsorships, regardless of the size of your brand.

The possibility of landing a sponsorship deal rises when your social media platforms are in very niche and technical markets. Another possibility for sponsorship money arises when you use some very complicated products to produce the content for your platforms. Service providers are increasingly paying social media influencers to demonstrate their products through their channels.

In these business dealings, you receive a set amount of money to lease them some aspect of your brand for them to demonstrate how their products work. Of course, you retain your role as a presenter, but you become a mouthpiece for their marketing content. This can be anything from the graphics you use to make your content to the dresses you wear, but in whatever scenario, your content will be focused on displaying the best of a business' products. So you will probably be asked to draw attention to the aspects of your content that have been produced using the sponsor's product.

Getting sponsored is somewhat of a failsafe money making technique. In most cases, you will find that your sponsor also pays to get your content to more people through adverts. As they seek a wider reach for their marketing content, they will also be helping to take your brand to even more people. However, you must understand that sponsorship is almost exclusively available to influencers who use videos to produce their content. Only video content gives you the dynamism to talk up a product and at the same time communicate with your followers without compromising either of these things.

Monetizing your gags

Sometimes, you can even truncate your video content and offer it out to sponsors. For example, if you have a running gag in all your content, you can insert a "presented by" tag. Because running gags are usually the part in which your followers are most interested, you can get a very good deal on it. I have seen just one vlogger who has done this, so it is very new. It also calls for a clearly identifiable running gag that your fans absolutely adore.

But you must be sure to keep the sanctity of your brand even while you make money off the important parts of it such as the running gags. You must not sell the soul of your business. You must stick to your brand identity.

Becoming the Standard of Excellence

I will go back to the movie industry to make my point on this revolutionary idea. You have seen them, those short opinions, often five-letter or even less, on the trailer of every new movie – the critics' opinion. These people determine the success of a movie to a very huge extent. Even if a studio's marketing department manages to rouse the public's interest and perform well at the box office, movies that were panned by critics rarely do well in awards –arguably the place where real success is actually made.

Now, I know that many books teach you how to market one product in the industry without offending others, who, understandably, might be future clients. So, in whatever endorsement or sponsorship deal you get, you always leave a small percentage of commitment behind. It shows in the passion with which you produce content and recommend a product. But what if you only marketed products that you really believed in to your followers? The marketers will have to battle it out amongst themselves to flip your opinion and earn your endorsement. Influencers shun this strategy- probably because it takes a lot more time- but it has massive potential for building your brand even more and increasing your ability to make money.

The first step in this strategy is to get into a niche market with many players and establish your brand as the most authoritative. It is imperative that you become the go-to person for internet users in that niche, so be sure to make only the best of recommendations. Understand all products in the industry inside out, gather market intelligence, and basically just command the loyalty (and the opinions) of users. Businesses will not care what you think if you are not the one shaping opinions. But when you become the opinion shaper, when your word determines whether or not their products perform well, then you become a very influential social media influencer indeed!

This is how small players capture lucrative sponsorship deals. Because you have made yourself the ultimate consumer and have the backing of thousands of hopefully similarly dedicated users, the producers will be fighting to become your darlings. Instead of hunting for your sponsorship deals, you let the companies hunt you down themselves. Now that is real influence!

Merchandising

I have seen some social media influencers who created very strong brands making some very good money off them by selling t-shirts, bags, bangles, and a ton of other merchandise. Now, if there is one monetization avenue that is discriminating about the strength of the brand, that would be merchandising. The process of creating a merchandise-worthy brand is much like the process outlined in this book. However, you make a habit of wearing merchandise with a specific type of design. As you become more and more influential and as you convert your fans into super fans, you will see the demand for similar merchandise rise. It is then that you can endeavor to create official merchandise and sell it to your fans.

The great thing about merchandising is that the money you earn is all yours. Instead of relying on other businesses for your cash, you create an avenue to make money directly from your followers through good old-fashioned product exchange business. However, you must meet a few standards to exploit the wondrous world of merchandising fully. First off, you must customize your social media platforms into points of sale. Second, you must create a strong support infrastructure for your business outside of social media. Third, you will have to resort to influence marketing to drive sales for your merchandising business.

Become a Point of Sale

The process of converting your social media platforms into points of sale requires quite a bit of work. First off, you must unlock merchant selling on Facebook, Instagram, Twitter, and all other accounts on which your brand has a presence. With merchandising, you will be forced to start thinking like a retailer and operating your brand as such. First things first, the chatbots that we mentioned earlier are critical. A social site like Facebook provides the tools necessary to run a shop. Make sure that you talk up your brand there. On other sites, create strategic content to sell your merchandise.

One very effective strategy for selling merchandise is to advertise (as surreptitiously as possible) on the header image. This way, people will be reminded about your merchandising side-hustle in a non-intrusive way every time they visit any of your platforms. However, you must be prepared to lose some of your marketability as a general influencer. This is especially likely when your platforms seem to be too engaged in self-promotion to do any promotional work for other businesses.

Maybe in the beginning, be willing to give up some

of your power as an influencer marketer. As you turn your attention to your own business, it is inevitable that you will lose some of your focus insofar as promoting other businesses is concerned. Merchandising is hands down one of the most effective ways of diversifying your interests as a social media influencer. The income that you will be generating there will boost the income you make from all your other endeavors and make your business even more profitable.

Creating a Network for Your Business

Creating a successful merchandising operation requires that you establish very strong ties with the people who work in that area. And just because your business is based on social media and the Internet does not mean that you have to stick to Internet sales alone. Just as with getting businesses with which to establish influencer-marketing relations, successful social media influencers realize that their efforts offline have as big an impact on their brand as their efforts online. Just because your money comes from social media does not mean that you cannot make some of it in traditional institutions. You can leverage your position and your influence to get very good deals with brick and mortar stores that use the Internet to sell. This allows you to reach a bigger market and sell a lot more. Moreover, because these businesses have been dealing with retail sales a lot longer, they can probably do a better job in the manufacturing, pricing, delivery, and inventory management aspects of the business.

Leveraging Other Influencers

As an influencer, you will inevitably meet with numerous other influencers in and outside your industry. These people command their own massive followings and can probably give you access to a larger market. Create your own affiliate marketing operation and give other influencers a commission for every piece of merchandise sold through their channels. As long as you take care of your own bottom line, you will increase sales quite substantially.

Use Your Influence to Move into Dropshipping

The world of retail has recently been disrupted by a trend known as dropshipping. In dropshipping, a vendor connects the customer with the producer, facilitating the sale but not handling the product physically. All you need to succeed as a dropshipper is a niche market. Because you are buying directly from the producer and there are no middlemen, you can sell your stuff at a cheaper price. This is the main draw of dropshipping. Now, the one thing that most dropshippers struggle with is expanding their reach to the prospective market. Dropshippers struggle a lot to break the market, even using social media to advertise their products. In fact, if you do not make the move into dropshipping, you will probably work with a dropshipping enterprise at one point, selling them your influencer marketing packages.

However, as a social media influencer, you do not have to worry about that! You already have a dedicated following. Many social media influencers shy away from dropshipping because they feel that they would be betraying their brand. But this is simply not true! For one, people will always be more loyal to the person who saved them money or otherwise made their life easier at some point. Just make sure to stick to the 70/20/10 rule and only promote products that align with your brand. When you do this, the fact that you bring the best deals to your followers will only boost their liking of you. Moreover, the fact that you have a whole virtual store at your control gives you an edge over other influencers.

You can include a link to your e-shop on your platforms and mention the fact that your followers can get great deals there. This is paramount. You must show your followers how they will benefit by buying from your shop. It beats trying to convince them to buy to support your channel as a sort of pity buy. I have seen people try this and it crashes quickly. At some point, even your most ardent follower will grow tired of supporting you all for your sake. Show them how buying from you is the best idea. Exploit the camaraderie that your channels create between you and them. Keep taking care of their interests (or simply just selling everything in that manner) and you will make a lot more headway. And while you are at it, throw in a few coupons and discount vouchers to the people who visit your site from your social media platforms. This incentive works wonders to bring in new followers while at the same time boosting your store's sales.

Do not take the move into dropshipping lightly. It requires a lot more work than most people give it credit for. Sure, a lot of the work involved in dropshipping like finding a niche and establishing a following will be covered during the early stages of your social media influencer career, but you will still need to go out of your way to succeed here. You will have to multitask while setting up your shop, and the process of finding the best deals for your shop and dealing with producers, delivery, and customers will take up a huge chunk of your time. However, there is a lot of money to be made in dropshipping. It is another great opportunity to diversify from influencer marketing and make some good money with a lot less competition.

Intelligence Generation

Businesses are always hunting for intelligence on how to fulfill their customers' needs even better. They give out surveys, they pay consultancy firms, and they use their own social media accounts. But these avenues are not always successful. And even where they are successful, they will always be open to new suggestions. Now, social influencers are ideally positioned to benefit directly from this phenomenon. You see, in your niche, you work as an intermediary between producers and consumers. So if your brand deals in gaming consoles and equipment, you will be hearing from tens of thousands of followers about their frustrations with the products that exist in the market.

There are also tools that you can use to gather more information. In fact, I stumbled upon this idea while creating a poll intended to inform by content generation on Instagram. As thousands of my followers answered my poll, I realized that I was easily the only person who spent all my time listening to consumers' concerns about the products they used. I realized that as a social media influencer, we are all perfectly positioned to collect market intelligence. Producers can then use this information to improve their products, which in turn means that customers will get their needs fulfilled.

The good news is that you can collect, process, and sell this data. Possibly sell it at a premium too, if you find the right people. Moreover, if you do it right, you will take your place at the forefront of innovations in your industry. Not only does this bring a lot more prestige to your brand, you will be a prime candidate for lucrative endorsement deals.

But to get to a place where you can actually make an impact, you must first know the kind of information that your industry struggles to find about their products. You must then find the right tools to gather said information and process it. With all this in place, establish a system of open communication to enable you to listen to your followers. Keep in mind that information is power and if you want to accumulate any of it as a social media influencer, you must work for it.

Use Events

Businesses use events to connect with their customers. Professional gatherings such as trade conventions bring together people with similar interests. This is where social influencers come in. If your audience is part of the target market for an event, the organizers can ask you to help drum up attendance through your different channels. When monetizing events to which you are invited, you have to back it up with actual numbers from your followers showing up. Organizers will respect you more and hire your services again if you help make their first event a success by bringing in the numbers. But if your followers trust you enough and show up for you when you ask them to, you can make this a very versatile income source for your business.

Best Practices

Monetization is the ultimate goal for social media influencing. You want to become influential enough that you actually make some money off of it. And after all you had to do in creating the brand and growing an audience, monetization is something that is worth doing right. In this section, we will look at some of the few things that you can do to increase the potential of your social influencing career making you money.

1. Diversify: This is the most important lesson you will ever learn about monetization. The rule to follow is that you should not get more than 50% of your income from a single source. Instead, mix them up and try to make some money off every avenue that is available to you.

2. Do more than you think you should: Many influencers work from a sense of accomplishment and entitlement whereby they expect to be approached with the deals that will make them profitable social influencers. You must be willing to go out of your way to attract advertisers to your platforms. Alternatively, you can build a brand with the potential for merchandising and dropshipping operations. When you do that, you will have reduced your reliance on other businesses for your success right off the bat.

3. If monetization does not work, go back to the first and second parts of this guide and check there. If you created a strong enough brand and worked hard enough to attract followers, then you must succeed in making money out of them. Between the businesses that will come to you looking to exploit your influence and the ones that you can start independently (merchandising,

dropshipping, and intelligence gathering), you should have no trouble making money.

4. Keep learning: social media influencing and marketing are two industries that are always in constant change. If you do not keep up with these changes, you will find yourself sidelined and struggling to make money. If you cannot become the source of disruption in the industry, then make sure that you are among the first people to learn about innovations and to introduce them to your operation.

5. Become a mentor to new influencers. The knowledge you accumulate over the course of your social media influencing career is power. But it will only benefit you if you use it to help new entrants into the industry. Many people frown upon that advice because after all, these are the people who will be trying to unseat you in a few years. But that would only happen if you stopped grinding and making your brand better. If you are

confident in your skills as a social media influencer, you will take the opportunity of teaching others to improve your own skills. And if you can get them to pay for it, make a few buck while you are at it.

Part 4: Mistakes to Avoid

Becoming an influencer requires that you optimize your brand, audience connection, and monetization. Take risks, capitalize on every opportunity, and set the trends. But you must be careful not to mess it all up. A single mistake in the branding, audience building, or monetization part can be very costly to a social media influencer's career. In this section, we will cover the most dangerous mistakes in all three areas.

While Creating the Brand

Creating and maintaining your brand identity takes up nearly half of all the work that you will do. In the same way, your brand determines the level of profitability that you can reach. You simply cannot afford to make a mistake in designing a brand identity. In this chapter, we will focus on unraveling some of these mistakes. Because knowing about them (and how to avoid them) is absolutely critical for success in social media influencing.

Lacking a Clear Purpose

A social media influencer who does nothing but gather followers, post stuff, and harvest the likes will always come through as being vain. You can go some way, you can even garner a respectable following, but you will not get to the same level of success as someone with a purpose. This becomes especially critical when you are trying to attract sponsors and advertisers. Most businesses would pick someone with similar values and a good following over someone with a huge following but who does not share their values.

Think about the impact that you would like to create in your niche market. However small it might be, it could be the difference between success and failure. This is especially so when the businesses in your industry are heavily branded. A strong brand always seeks a strong brand. And when this happens, the strength must be in those shared values between them.

Not being authentic

Authenticity is something that everyone, including people in social media, crave. People want to see a part of them reflected in you – that is why we listen to music and watch movies. They all represent a part of us. It is the same for social media. This is the reason why some sections of the Internet bunch together and share information between them. It is all about relating. It is about finding shared values in another person and the opportunity to be yourself.

This is crucial for a social media influencer. To appeal to your target market, you must be authentically you, whatever "you" might be. Remember I talked about crafting a branded personality. This works when you are dealing with a very niche market and you think that sharing every aspect of your life might distract your followers from that purpose. But even in that case, you must be careful to stick to your brand personality. Do not be sidetracked and start mixing it up just out of the blue. You will end up disorienting your followers and probably damaging the identity you worked so hard to create.

Jumping the Grunt Work

Before you start your brand, you must do your homework and get yourself oriented to the state of your target market. Even if you consider yourself an expert, learn everything about what others in the industry are doing. Is there potential for a new entrant? And what opportunities are available for you to exploit? How can you make yourself stand out from other players in the same niche? And most importantly, what is the potential for money-making and who are the people that you need to impress to get that money?

This is called the grunt work. It is a lot less fun than the actual influencing, but it is critical if you want your brand to be profitable later on. It would be very tragic if you did all the work of creating a brand and gaining an audience only to find that there are no opportunities to make money later on.

Creating a Weak Brand

The brand you create must be strong enough to attract people and to compete with other influencers in your industry. It must also have the potential for monetization through merchandising, which is usually the hallmark of strong brands. And the only reason why people would be interested in a brand enough to buy branded merchandise is if the brand stood for something about them that they loved. This is where the brand values and your purpose really come in handy. If your purpose is simply to have followers and give them a name, then you will probably not do so well. But if you stand for, say, tirelessly grinding in business and entrepreneurship, or if you represented unrelenting commitment to working out or swimming, people would buy into those ideals.

A strong brand requires confidence, self-assurance, and dedication. You have to be the best at what you do. You must make sure everyone knows that, and you must try to get others to replicate you. This way, you form a community. If you decide to explore the idea of merchandise later on, it will just be the bond that ties you and your followers (who are already a community) even closer together.

Establishing Your Brand in a Dead-end Niche

Not all the things that excite you are very popular. Sometimes, you will discover that what you love is simply not popular enough to make you famous. This should not be along the process of establishing your social influencing career. Do your research early on, identify niches with potential, and only explore those ones. I have seen people make the mistake of thinking that they can explore an unpopular topic and make people interested in it enough to make money off it. And 100% of the time, I have seen these people fail. Do not attempt to make it in a dead-end niche, because it is impossible to make it there. Even if you might convince enough people to get excited about your ideas, chances are that there are no businesses to collaborate with you and make you some money. Your efforts could be all for nothing.

Ignoring the Competition

Whichever niche you get into, there will always be people making waves there. And while you should definitely not let them discourage you, you must acknowledge them. You must look at them and determine the areas in which they are failing and endeavor to plug these holes. As you start out, try not to meet them head-on. The impact might throw you off. Instead, gather your followers and build your audience before facing off against them. When you start worrying about the competition very early, you will have no time to build yourself. You need to keep one eye on them and another on the goal – until you are ready to take the war to them and take them down.

Mistakes to Avoid in Building (and maintaining) an Audience

A good brand without a good audience would be a huge letdown. So, in this section, let us look at all the mistakes you could be making that might be bringing your social influencing career down.

Having Inactive Profiles

Any platform worth hosting an account is a platform worth hosting an active account. It does not matter if a social network has little activity or potential, or if you find it less exciting and thus engage in it less. You owe it to yourself, your brand, and your audience to keep updating all your platforms on a regular basis. This is why it is advisable to open accounts on just a few social networks. It is better to be active on two or three platforms. If you have difficulties keeping up, narrow it down.

Another mistake that could be just as deadly as inactivity is the irregular updating of content. In fact, it is best to have pre-prepared content and timed posts, especially for those ardent followers who consume everything you post. For example, if a person can count on you to release the video that they watch on their daily commute to or from work, then they will become even more dedicated.

Posting Controversial Content

This might seem to go against the idea I floated earlier that you should stand for something, so let me take this opportunity to clarify that standing for something does not mean creating controversy. Controversial topics – like religion, race relations, and political ideologies – will only succeed in distracting your audience from the true purpose of your brand. And if your brand is aimed at creating controversy, then make sure that you do so in a respectful and non-offensive manner.

Deviating from Your Brand

One thing you must always keep in mind is that your followers follow you because of who you are and what you represent. If you do something contrary to that, they will probably feel alienated. There is no telling what might transpire if that happens. However, you can expect to lose a good chunk of any influence you have. Your brand must be your compass in everything you do as a social influencer. Whoever you say you are on that bio, stick to that.

Some of the most effective brand management practices I have seen include a five-point checklist with which you vet all original and shared content on your channels. The only content that should appear on your timeline should be that which meets at least four of the five checkpoints.

Lacking Original Content

You have probably seen those accounts that have so much reposted content that you cannot tell what material is original and which of it represents the brand's identity. The best way to connect to your audience is by creating original content. This is what endears you to them. When you forego original content, you forego the best chance you have of making a meaningful impression.

The same goes for the volume of original content on your channels. There is a trend among social media influencers of moving away from that "influencer" tag and becoming more of a "creator". This change has been taking place gradually over the last few years because businesses are also shifting their marketing strategies to focus more on original content. Your ability to create quality original content determines the level of attention you attract from marketers.

Getting too Personal

Authenticity is one of the most important qualities for a brand, but you must avoid making it too personal. And I know that this is a controversial topic, but not many people enjoy feeling like they are being an audience to someone else's life drama. This is why engagement in a social network like Facebook has been dropping while Instagram blows up. Keep the personal drama to a minimum and remember that your followers are not an audience to your life. Unless it adds some real value to their own lives, they will gradually grow less interested until they drop off altogether.

Ignoring the Competition

The competition is a very important part of your career as a social media influencer. You will only get the followers that they fail to impress or that they lose and the same thing goes for you. For this reason, you simply cannot ignore the activity of your competitors. The key is to make sure that you get all their disillusioned followers and lose none of yours to them. If you ignore the competition and they start giving their followers something of value that you do not, you will lose them. There will always be follow battles between influencers in the same industry. As long as you make sure that you are on the gaining side of these battles, you will do great. But if you find yourself losing, then it might be time to re-evaluate your brand strategy and the content that you are creating. If both are okay, then consider promoting yourself a lot more than you are doing now.

Mistakes to Avoid in Monetizing Your Brand

Monetization is the essence of social influencing. If you cannot make money out of your social media presence, then there is no difference between you and billions of other users. You have to set yourself apart as the person who makes money out of it. And to do this, you have to run a pretty tight ship when it comes to brand identity and getting an audience. In this section, we will cover the common mistakes that thwart many influencers' ambitions of making money from social media.

Promoting the Wrong Way

There are two types of social media brands that never reach their greatest potential; one that promoted too much and one that does not promote enough. It is very interesting that you can go wrong by doing too much of something that you should be doing anyways, but this is the case with social influencing. When you are constantly bombarding your followers with pleas to buy this or that, they will soon grow disillusioned and stop following you. Instead, focus on the kind of advertising that does not interfere with your followers' interaction with your content. If you have to sell directly to them, then do so for a few days every month.

On the other hand, you cannot make money if you do not do enough promotion. Even your most ardent fans will need some prompting to engage with your promotional content and, even more importantly, to act on it.

So if you are selling some merchandise or you are running a dropshipping business on the side, be sure to share that information and to give your followers all the tools they need to act on it. However, do not go too far and bombard them with promotional content all the time. Find the perfect balance and stick to it.

Failing to Engage with Potential Buyers

I understand that you receive a ton of trolling messages and flirting messages from secret admirers, but should that deter you from replying to those genuine messages from interested customers? The answer is an emphatic no. The worst thing you can do is fail to engage someone who has some interest in something you are selling and converting him or her into a buyer. Attend a sales course if you must, but you must figure out the best way to convert every interest into a buying decision. Your sales skills might actually be the difference between success and failure. Polish them every day and make sure that you unleash them on all your followers for an even more lucrative brand.

Failing to Collect Data

So you have decided to use a few thousand dollars to market yourself. Did you track the impact of that campaign or are you just as clueless about its impact as you were before spending all that money? Many influencers get in the habit to plough a fixed amount of their earnings back into the business through promotions and adverts. However, they fail to track the impact of their marketing campaigns.

When this money does not work as well as it should, they remain clueless. You must optimize your spending and make sure that every dollar that you put into the business is actually bringing more back. Whichever service you advertise on will usually have tracking tools. Use them to decide the best way to advertise.

Other forms of data that you can collect to increase the profitability of your business is user data from your followers. Every day that you engage with them, ensure that you come out with information that you might share with other businesses for some money.

Selling

Your role as a social influencer is to fulfill the wishes of your followers. The difference between selling and fulfilling wishes is that the former just pushes products and services while the latter listens and gives the audience what the audience wants. Be the one who fulfills your followers' dreams instead of just pushing products that they might not be interested in.

Once Again, Ignoring the Competition

Because you will be fighting for the same marketing deals, the same customers, and the same dollars, the competition comes into play in the monetization process more than anywhere else. If you cannot hold your own against the strongest players in the industry, you will end up missing all the great opportunities for making money in social influencing.

The best way to beat the competition is aiming to be the best you can be and building on that to rise to the top... and keep rising.

Conclusion

So there you have it! The ultimate step-by-step guide to building your personal brand and growing a business online in a simple three-part process comprising of branding, growing your audience, and monetizing the whole operation. It is within these steps that your success as a social influencer will be determined. If you can do all three perfectly, through whatever combination of qualities and actions, you will definitely succeed. In this chapter, we will run through the whole book and summarize the three parts in short order.

First, you create a brand. The most important thing in branding is to make it pop. It is crucial that you stand out from all other influencers in the market. To do this, you make sure that your brand is personable, authentic, and charismatic. And as you do all this, make sure that you have thought through the whole process. A successful social influencer is only recognized when they start making money, but they are made through, more than anything else, proper branding. So think of your brand as your business, determine the avenues for making money that are open to you, and create a plan of how you will reach there. Operating the social influencing operation like a business goes a long way in driving profitability because you will be more interested in doing everything the right way.

The second thing you do is build an audience. Building an audience starts with target mapping. Here, you create the ultimate follower's profile, determine what sites you are more likely to find him or her, and then go to work attracting as many of them as possible. To create a good connection between your different social networks, you integrate them using similar usernames and links. To build an audience, you must create the right content for them. You must decide whether that would be images, videos, text, or infographics. The most effective and versatile of these mediums is video. I highly recommend that you use them. But, more importantly, customize your content for every social network and do not send links to any of them. Give every channel where you have a profile the same level of attention as all other channels.

Social influencers thrive on super fans. These people follow you on every social network, share the same values as your brand, and engage with all your content. After deciding on what medium you will use to reach your audience, you should work to convert your fans into super fans. Your do this by appealing to the fantasies, and engaging with them.

You must also do everything you can to increase the reach of your content. If you are posting on a social network, find out the times of the day when there is the highest level of engagement. And if you are having trouble connecting with your followers, do not be afraid to pay for a wider reach through paid adverts and influencer follows.

The final step in building a career in social influencing entails finding the businesses that will give you money to sell their products or services to your followers. You must develop your sales skills because businesses usually pay according to the level of penetration that your platforms give them. To diversify and create new streams of income for your business, consider selling merchandise goods, starting a dropshipping operation, or collecting and selling market data to the companies in your niche market.